Wandering Journey

Copyright (c) 2005, Lori Cahill
All rights reserved. Printed in the U.S.A.

No part of this publication may be reproduced or transmitted in any form or by any means, electronic or mechanical, including photocopy, recording or any information storage and retrieval system now known or to be invented, without permission in writing from the publisher, except by a reviewer who wishes to quote brief passages in connection with a review written for inclusion in a magazine, newspaper or broadcast.

Published in the United States by
Beckham Publications Group, Inc.
P.O. Box 4066, Silver Spring, MD 20914

ISBN: 0-931761-08-5
10987654321

Wandering Journey

Poems

Lori Cahill

PUBLICATIONS GROUP, INC.
Silver Spring

Contents

Amazed	1
No Limitations	3
My Thorn	5
Bloom Where You're Planted	7
Our Response	9
Spider Webs	11
A Bruised Reed	12
We Are Not At Home	14
A Humble Heart	16
Tip Of The Iceberg	18
The Other Sin	20
Too Guilty For God	22
A Low Spirit; A Call For Help	24
It's A God Thing	26
Our Own Backyard	27
A Salvation Package	28
Halftime	30
The Bell Rings	32
Desperate	34
Some People See	35
When It Hurts	36
What Do I Pray?	37
The Ultimate Gift	38
Our Choice	39
Words For My Friend	40
Peacefully Finding God's Peace	41
Knocking On Heaven's Door	42
Bearing Fruit	44
What In The World Are We Doing?	46
Sunday Morning	48
Thought Patterns	50
Strongholds	52
Searching	54
Are You Calling?	56
Guests?	58
The Ripple	59
Purity	61
Another's Strings	62
The Source	64
A Prayer From A Sinner	65
Hurting	67
The Restlessness For Thirst	69
Lighthouse	70

No Harm	72
Contentment	74
Be Where You Are!	76
Short Term Living	78
What If?	79
Boiler Maker's Daughter	81
Trivial Pursuit	83
Forgiven	85
The Prodigal	87
The Prodigal's Elder	89
Global Warming	90
Looking Over Your Shoulder	91
The Last Time	92
Turning The Other Cheek	93
In The Blink Of An Eye	94
Putting It All Together	96
When Christ Is In Your Heart	98
The Warmth Of The Son	100
Eternity	101
You Can Always Look Up	102
Surrender	103
Grace	104
Redemption	105
Just Because	107
To Turn Or Shake	108
Ignoring God	110
Lukewarm	112
In It Not Of It	114
The Crutch	116
Our Mission	117
Expectations	119
Sovereignty	121
Two Lives	123
Wondering	125
Pity Parties	127
Thanks Be To God	129
Because	131
The Perfect Christmas	133
Love	135
What Was It Like?	136
On This Day	137
What If Jesus Had Not Come?	139
Thirty Three Years	140

Amazed

It takes so much to amaze us, in this high tech world today,
Gadgets and gizmos of technology, for which we gladly pay.

We numb so very quickly, it soon becomes an old hat.
Looking for bigger and better, or what is "Where it's at"

We do the same with God's world, His blessings and His gifts,
We take them all for granted, as our life, it quickly sifts.

The years go by, we start to think, what we have, we do deserve!
We worked so hard, and spent our time; we hoard, and keep reserves.

And then the Bible stories, become old, we feel worn out,
The virgin birth, the water to wine, the mute, who could now shout.

And miracles that happen within our lives today,
We somehow try to justify, by what we do or say!

Life becomes a quickening blur; we're spinning round and round,
Not stopping to appreciate, sometimes, just hearing sounds.

Our problem is we overload, with stuff and things we spree,
We've forgotten how amazing blessings are for you and me.

The trees, the sun, and ocean deep, the child's smile, the wind, the rain.
The gentle touch of loving hands, of deliverance from sick or pain.

The hymn, the Word, the organ tune, the Bible stories we know,
The miracles, the awesomeness, of how God's love does flow.

The cross, the nails, the empty tomb, the angels, and the songs they sing.
The leper healed, the deaf that hear, the joy that healing brings!

We need to fall upon our knees, Our God -- is so amazing!
Open your eyes and hear it all, to feel the Spirit blazing.

Awake your mind, and hear the song, clean your heart and mind today,
Be amazed by your Father's works; see the light, His Word, the Way.

Wandering Journey

Awake the nerves, rid the numb revitalize your senses,
Listen quietly, see and feel, God's presence in all tenses.

How amazing is our God, the song of grace, so free.
Christ has saved us, the Spirit lives, Oh God, please help me see.

Amen

No Limitations

With God there are no limitations
No walls or boundaries to face.
His ultimate power is unending
And so is His power and grace.

With God there are no limitations
On healing the sick or the worn
Of new life given to the weary
Of hope for the tired and the torn.

There's no limit on God's love forever
He knows each of His children so well
Our thought, our fears, and our worries
Our hearts and our minds, He can tell.

He knows what's happening in our life.
He knows when we're tempted to sin.
He knows when we're touched by the spirit,
And all of the places we've been.

There's no limit on his creating
New life. He brings every hour
Children, His beautiful children.
Individually created by his power.

His unlimited creation of this planet
The stars, the moon, and the sun.
Plants, trees, and the balance of nature
The cycles of life, How they run!

All in a balanced perfection
It's from our God, the divine plan
The universe continues with no falter
The awesomeness of this great span.

And yet in His great power
He knows and hears each as we pray.
Personally seeing our pain and joy
Knows our heart and thoughts every day.

God has no limits! He is awesome.
We cannot truly understand
Our human minds don't seem big enough,
To know the power of his hand.

With God, there are no limitations
Dimensions we cannot conceive
No limit to His greatest power
And the glorious blessings received.

My Thorn

Oh God, How this thorn hurts!
Its constant pain I feel
Sometimes the pain subsides a bit
But I know it's always real.

I've had other thorns in my life.
But they didn't hurt this much.
And time would heal, they'd fade away.
And I could move and touch.

But this one is so frightening.
It brings me to my knees.
I pray to God, take it away!
Take it out now, dear God please!

Just when I think it's gone away.
And I think I have no pain.
It knocks me to my knees again
Like a hurricane wind and rain.

Oh God, I think I understand
The part where Paul did so plead.
To have the thorn removed for good
From the pain and agony freed.

But you told him that would not be
Your grace is all sufficient
And that He must continue on
His journey, he must be patient.

Is that why this thorn I cannot pluck
From the wound so very sore?
So your grace is guiding, comforting me
But the thorn keeps me knocking at your door.

Oh God, I call to you today.
I need a dose of love
To numb the pain this thorn causes,
I need strength and hope from above.

And if this thorn with me must stay!
Whatever is the plan!
Dear God, grant me grace to go
Sufficient for my life span.

Help me turn this thorn of pain
Transform it to a flower.
That will mature my soul and heart
With blooming spiritual power.

That looks up in the sun of warmth
And soaks up all the rays,
And drinks up water of life from you
And grows each earthly day.

This thorn will help me care and share
And empathy will grow
So beauty and wisdom will come forth
And your heavenly influence show.

Oh God, I thank you for your grace,
Your Fatherly love and power.
I trust you God, with my life
Turn this thorn into a flower.

Amen

Bloom Where You're Planted

The flowers don't complain or gripe
When springtime comes around
They are happy where they're planted
And blossoms come abound.

The apple, cherry, and peach trees
Full of flowers and blooms
They don't hold back their beauty,
Because they don't like their place or room!

And so with us, upon this earth
Should follow the flowers way
And bloom where we are planted
And do it yes! Today.

We may be caught in a wheelchair
Or dealing with a sickness so mean.
But there is always room for thankfulness.
From our Father and Jesus we lean!

We may be poor and struggling
The budget may be tight!
But we can share our love and joy!
We can share our light!

We may have lost a loved one.
To death, oh, what a sting!
But that empty spot within your heart!
Can wonderful memories bring.

No matter what is happening,
In your garden spot today,
Sunshine, toil, rain or shine
There is always a hopeful ray.

But we can always find a way
To bring forth and produce a flower!
Let your roots reach out and grasp
Unto our Father's power!

Soak in His love and sunshine,
And drink the words He's given!
And grow where you are planted.
And soon the buds are given.

Filled with love, peace, and hope
Buds ready to burst so soon.
Bring forth your blossoms of God's love,
And where you're planted, BLOOM!

Our Response

The tone of your voice, the words that you say
Makes such a difference in the walk of the day.

Your response, your face, the message you bear
Will show your apathy, or show that you care.

It can rip a heart, or crush a dream.
Encourage a thought or it can be mean.

Our response, our interactions to the world around,
Sometimes it would be better, if we make no sound.

For with a word ill spoken, we can cause much pain.
And destroy a spirit struggling to sustain.

And often those things so hurtfully said
Are because of our own problems, that has led

Us to be hurtful, selfish, and unkind.
Because we didn't deal with them, but kept them in mind.

Anxiety, fear, lack of self confidence too.
Causes us to lash out, the response we do!

Harmful hurt and pain to others around.
Because we are hurting, we hurt those surround.

We must deal with our sorrows, our cobwebs, and grief.
Our inadequate feelings and negative beliefs.

And then hold our tongue and think before we say,
Resist criticism and ruining someone's day.

Words that come forth, from our mouth from now on!
Should be honest and caring, a new type of song.

Of responses of love, responses that care
Words carefully spoken, words openly shared.

Wandering Journey

Remember that once those words are out and spoken.
Can lift a person up, or their heart may be broken.

So think before speaking, slow down before talk.
As it all will reflect, on this earthly walk!

Spider Webs

We hear people talk about them, they're lurking everywhere
In the corners and the closets, on our face and in our hair,
They come in all kinds or sizes; they can be large or small.
They can make us trip or stumble, and can stop us like a wall.

The sins of life are cobwebs; they hang around and grow
Clouding up our hallways, in life as we try to go.
It may be booze or pictures; not getting our things done,
Drugs or lust or dirty words; or things the world calls fun!

It may be harbored hatred; or quiet or bitter thoughts.
Jealousy or gossip; or what success has brought.

It can even be anger, at our heavenly God above
Because we don't get our way, and think He doesn't love,
They entangle and surround us; distort our mind and soul!
We think were fine! All is all right; but we're racking up a toll!

We may even see we need to clear, the webs that block our life!
We knock them down, but they come back; returning causing strife.
We cover and disguise them, sell help from books and talk,
Paying people to help us through, but in the webs we're locked.

Until we kill the spiders; the sin that keeps us down
We must remove the spider; for freedom to be found.

We must kill the spider! It's simple as can be!
Confess the sin, repent to God, that from webs you're freed.
Then a change will happen; the spirit will guide you through.
A new refreshing way of life; is found for me and you.

Don't put it off another day, not a minute or an hour.
Ask God to kill the spider now, filling you with heavenly power.
A new and bright day is dawning, new vision and fresh air
Of hope, eternal peace, and love; filled with God's eternal care!

A Bruised Reed

A bruised reed He will not break
He will not crush or crumble
A smoking flax he will not quench
So we must believe and be humble.

When times are hard and so oppressed
We're overcome with fear.
Overwhelmed with life and trials
About to explode with tears!

The stress, confusion, where's the sense?
Has madness throughout the world spread
Numbers live as if they don't care
Taking more than their daily bread.

We feel crushed, perplexed, and outnumbered
By the secular way of living.
Where are the morals, the common prayer?
Sharing, loving, and giving?

A smoking flax not quenched
A bruised reed not broken
Our God will lovingly guide us through
Follow the word He's spoken!

So awake daily with heavenly hope
And join in you Father's presence.
Pray often and read the divine word
And seek our Father's essence.

To rise above the worldly things,
A different perspective you'll see
A new hope in life, agape love
A future for you and me.

God will be with us, He understands
Our struggling fears and life.
He knows our pain and our confusion.
As we try to wallow through strife.

Wandering Journey

So when the news is frightening
And the world has gone insane.
Remember the reed not broken
And the smoking flax that flames.

We Are Not At Home

Daily we get up and through our day roam
Trying to find the perfect home.

A world of harmony, love, peace
A world where happiness doesn't cease.

But instead we see pain, lies, and deceit
Murdering, pollution, problems we meet.

Parents having children who don't really care
Addiction and torment, too much to bear.

And just while we're struggling to find our way
There is just so much to do! So much to pay.

We see glimpses of peace, and bits of light
And occasionally we sleep, soundly at night.

But we can't settle in, we can't settle down
It seems we just keep roaming around.

Why can't everyone love, why hate and despair?
Why can't we get along? Why not truly care?

But it doesn't happen, just look on the news!
Hurting and hating; so many lives to lose.

Remember Jesus said He has a mansion for you.
We're living here now, but traveling through.

This place is temporary; we're here for a while!
But when we walk our last earthly mile.

We will see a bright and new dimension
One with no pain, no hate, no tension.

Our new body and life will start in heaven.
Thanks be to God, for this he has given.

Wandering Journey

Each day is numbered that we live here on earth
God has it planned from the day of our birth.

This is a journey, and a temporary road
And remember God helps you carry the load.

Hang in there; we're heading for higher ground.
Take a day at a time! We're heaven bound.

A Humble Heart

As we journey, each day we live
There are things we learn in life.
One is that a prideful heart
Can cause pain, injury, and strife.

A puffed up mind of arrogance
Of "I can do it all"
"I'm handling this all by myself"
Will set you up to fall!

For though your day is going great!
The sun is shining bright.
A problem could be your next phone call
That turns your day to night!

A death, an illness, an injury,
A marriage heart to keep
As pride and thinking you don't need God!
Will result in sorrow! So deep!

Our future is unknown each day!
To each of us we go
We don't know what tomorrow brings
If the day will be high or low!

But a humble heart keeps you true!
To your loving God in heaven.
You know you can't make a day of life.
Without the grace He has given!

And when you cling tightly to God,
The fear and anxieties fade
And when the rough times hit you hard
There is Jesus, a level path He's made!

So when the times are rough going!
He is holding on to you
Sometimes He is even carrying
Your brokenness, pain and blues.

Remember to keep humility
And go out and wash some feet
Keep a simple plan of life
That God's plans for you…you'll meet!

And put the prideful heart away
Bragging, and tooting your own horn!
For the Gracious Hands of God,
You can truly be reborn.

When I have the tendency,
To say "Look what I have done!"
Remember it's all God's precious gifts
That allows you to live and run!
So humbly on your knees do pray
Tell God thank you for all and all!
Ask Him to guide and bless your path
So you may follow His call!

Tip of the Iceberg

We only see a tiny tip of the whole picture don't you see,
We only see just glimpses, of blessings for you and me.

We hurry here, and hurry there, with our taxes and daily living,
We see so little how we are blessed, and how our Father's giving.

Oh, we thank Him for our daily meals, and thank Him for each day,
For food and clothes, and friends about, for family, yes we say!

But that is only the tip of the iceberg, there are so many
Things He gives.

The thankful list is unending, it continues daily as we live.

Reach down and feel your pulse beats, think how your brain
Does store,

The knowledge, thoughts, and all you do, Oh yes! There is so
Much more.

The laws of nature, the earth we live, the life from big to small
The heavens above, the earth below, waters that flow and fall.

To love, to care, to feel the need, to be there for someone.
To have the same love given back, no matter how it's done.

The Bible, words of prophets past, Old Testament and New,
The Spirit of God that works in us, to guide in what we do.

The gift of life, each so unique, God created each on this earth,
The temple for our given soul, He gives our life, at birth.

And somehow when tough times appear, struggles and toils in life,
God helps us to find wisdom and strength, to mature and preserve
Through strife!

Our blessings Oh! We cannot count, they're infinite don't you see,
Take in a breath; enjoy your life, the gift given to you and me.

Wandering Journey

Don't just look at the tip of the iceberg, reach out to find and explore,
Blessings from God, there everywhere, simply look outside
The door!

The Other Sin

As we travel the road to maturing,
In our Christian life today
We've crossed the bridge of acceptance
Of Jesus, our sins to pay.

We know what's right, the things that are wrong,
The commandments we understand
We seldom lie, and do not steal,
Trying to follow and take God's hand.

We do not kill, or take God's name
In vain, we try not to do!
Trying to adhere to the written laws
Given for me and you!

But what about another look
The things we do not do!
Opportunities that come in life
That can be a sin for us too!

Looking the other way sometimes
At someone who is in need
Not giving all we're meant to give,
Because of simple greed.

Putting out a spark of hope,
Because we didn't walk the extra mile,
To reach out and grab a hand,
But instead, contemplated for a while.

Not taking time for a lost soul,
Who simply needed a bit of time.
A word, a smile, or gentle touch,
Or maybe just a dime.

Yes, these are sins, just as bad,
Confess and recognize.
And when you feel the need to move,
The next time, you'll be surprised.

Wandering Journey

Letting the Spirit really flow
Throughout your soul and mind.
Enables you to act upon,
Those around you that you find.

Lend some help, a smile, and a prayer
Contribute to a cause!
Your heart will move, you'll do your best
Not hesitating for a pause.

So remember that is not just a list,
Of things you should not do,
To follow God, to live the life
Step forward, let God work through you!

Too Guilty For God

We carry so much with us
In bags you cannot see,
The baggage is so heavy,
You'd like to set it free.

They're hang-ups from the past
Guilt that is stuffed away
So awful and so dirty,
We know that we must pay.

We try to keep that baggage
Away from those at church
You're sure that they would notice
As if displayed upon a perch.

Some people just couldn't handle it
At church or Sunday school
They'd think that I'm so dirty,
And that I've been a fool.

They all look so clean and nice
They'll find out where I've been,
The predicaments that encountered,
I wouldn't even tell a friend.

Stop right there for a minute!
Your thinking is all wrong
You need to turn it all around!
You need a fresh new song!

First, let go of the baggage,
The guilt that weighs you down,
Pray for cleansing from our God,
You'll soon lose that guilty frown.

Pray to be set free quickly.
To be clean and white as snow!
Clean every corner and hidden spot,
So clean, that you see a glow!

Wandering Journey

Now you've got the picture,
Your clean as clean can be!
God's given you a special gift,
And now you're set so free.

The next step is change your life,
Forever from this day!
Once Jesus enters, it's all new!
In what you do or say!

The Spirit works within you,
New ways and roads to go,
A plan written by your Father
For your life, Oh! It will show!

And now you find those at church,
They are sinners just like you.
All seeking for the answer,
Holding hands, as they pass through.

It is all a simple process,
It is written in the Book!
Accept the way; let God in your life
And from new eyes you'll look.

A Low Spirit: A Call For Help

It starts in the morning when you wake
You're tired and you don't want to move,
You don't know how you can get out of bed.
After all, there's nothing to prove.

You punch in on the clock daily,
You're always on time, never late
But your spirit is low and dragging,
And feels like your future may be your fate.

You don't remember when you last felt good!
Or had the energy to run
When you were excited about the day ahead,
Or felt looking forward to fun.

Everything seems foggy, nothing is clear
The days are not crisp or bright!
Your favorite time is lying down to bed,
And to sleep, and rest for the night.

You want to help so many out there
Your heart, it's in the right place. . .
You just seem to run out of energy and life.
It seems like you're losing the race.

And the needs of the world are countless
What can I do for this place?
There are too many problems, too much evil.
It's overwhelming, too much to face.

You know you believe in your Father
You know He cares and knows you.
But you wonder if He has time for your problems
As he has just so much to do.

What is happening! What's wrong with this picture?
This can't be the way that it goes.
I'm sinking in a pit little by little
Letting the darkness come from my foes.

Wandering Journey

The darkness, the cloud so dark and gloom
That is lingering from above
Taking away rays of sunshine and hope
Binding me as I reach out to love.

Oh! God! Light my way! A path for my feet
I've limited your strength and your power.
Open my eyes and remove these scales
Let me look to thy heavenly tower!

The devils deception, his slyest tool
Depression, dejection, so down
Not keeping our eye on heaven above
Not seeking the holy crown.

Oh! Forgive me, my Father, help me to see
To remove these bands from my chest
Renew my strength my hope from above!
I know now this is only a test.

I cry to you Father, I am so ashamed
For wallowing in the state that I've been.
Let me breathe and experience your awesome power
And overcome and defeat this sin.

It's A God Thing

The recovered alcoholic knows about it
The reborn Christian knows what it brings
The prisoner who's on a new
They know! *It's a God Thing*

The parent of a premature baby
The widow, who continues to sing.
The prostitute, who now has a family
They know, *It's a God Thing*

The girl who decided against abortion
And now, a sweet baby does sing,
The moment of union for the couple,
They know that *it's a God Thing*

The Downs Syndrome baby, born so quietly.
The parents hang onto the wing
Of the angel who opens their eyes to joy,
The child! *It's a God Thing*

The hopeless, no hope but bleak winter
Now sees a new world! It's like spring.
New attitude and hope for the future
They know *It's a God Thing*

Oh death, the sorrow, the pain!
The separation! The loss! The sting!
Then knowing, eternal life is waiting
Heaven! *It's a God Thing*

The list can continue forever
His power, to the world He does bring!
Our Father above, the Lord Jesus Christ!
The Spirit! *It's a God Thing*

Our Own Backyard

We see so much around us, so wicked and sad,
The world seems crazy, the pain produced so badly.

There is killing oh so frequent, cheating, lying, and deceit.
All from the love of money, impossible to defeat.

The innocent exploited, the guilty are set free.
Bending of the rules, designed for you and me.

Somehow in this confusion, we're to make a stand,
To uphold the word of God, and lend a hand.

But how can we in this chaos! It's confusing don't you see.
Where can I start? There's so much, I feel scared, and want to flee.

Sit calmly for a second; take in a deep breath and sigh,
Fall on your knees, and bow down to our God in the sky

For strength and courage, for an eagles view
What on this earth, is God's will for you.

Look in your backyard, His will is there,
You don't need to search, to find those in need of care
You won't fix the world, or change social trends
You can make a difference, in you, family, and friends.

Helping those close, in your neighborhood or school,
Your church, work, or family, if you let God rule.

To help you see clearly, you'll know what to do
You'll just do His will, not searching for clues.

Look in your backyard, to help and do God's will,
Bit by bit we make changes, His work it will fill.

Don't sit and wait for great calls, or search far away,
God has a plan-it's so close by, you can start today!

A Salvation Package

Are you tired of living in the same old way?
The old habits and grieves you bare?
The loads of life that get you down
And a burden with no one to share?

Tired of feeling the deck is stacked
And your card is never good?
The road you travel never smooth
And life never goes as it should.

The ruts you've dug are very deep
And you've got friends there to prove
That once they are dug, the hardened ruts
You cannot get out or move.

Well here is a ticket! A new way out!
Given specially just for you
A way to go! The air is pure!
And is not that hard to do!

Confront yourself, admit your wrongs
Stop denying, see the real thing
The road you're going is not right
So avoid going where it may bring!

Ask Jesus to forgive you now!
Invite him into your heart.
Pray to be cleansed, as white as snow
Pray now, to have a new start.

Then leave those ruts one by one!
Holding God's hand as you go,
Don't look back, keep your eyes ahead!
And soon a new light will show.

Pray for God's spirit to guide your way
To live for a new purpose and goals
To do his will and be free of ruts
To enlighten and penetrate you soul.

Now you're living, to do the will of God.
You know he is always by your side.
You hold his hand; He's in your heart
And through eternity, you will abide.

Halftime

There is a point in life
Where you finally slow down
You stop to look where you are going
And where your future bounds.

You take a breath, yes really breathe,
And find that all you have done
Doesn't bring the true happiness
That was intended by God's Son.

You've worked and struggled for what you own,
And punch in each day on the clock,
Scurrying along, doing the work,
Following the crowd, one in a flock.

You've worried, tossed, and turned at night
Trying to figure out solutions and ways
Saving, building to get all those dreams
And exhausted, at the end of your day.

You've climbed the ladder of success at work,
You're in charge of people and things,
You're proud of the plaques hanging on the wall
And all the prestige that they bring.

You've tried to straighten out some of the mess
That people around you have made
You've put out fires and helped them out
On the rocky paths that they've laid.

But something is missing, it's not right
It's the halftime of your life today
You know you've got to start a plan,
This is not the ticket or the way.

All of this is not important!
My priorities they're all mixed up!
I've been wasting my efforts on the wrong things
I've been drinking from the wrong cup!

Wandering Journey

My eyes need to be fixed on the Savoir
My goals need to be in His plan,
I've not loved, cared, or been humble
I've not given all that I can.

So take me, make me, and refresh me,
Set me on the right path and new way,
Help me to get motivated; refocus
To do the most with each day.

So my days that I live are not to worry
But trusting in God as I go
Seeking his guidance and plans for me
So the blessings can overflow.

And may the last half of my lifetime
Be joyful as I'm doing God's will.
May my heart and mind follow His way
And my soul continue to fill.

With goodness and close obedience
With seeking His work every day.
To share, teach, and reach out daily
To the others I meet on the way.

Create in me a clean heart, Father
And hold me close to Thy Hand
Use me as thine instrument, Father
May I do the best that I can.

The Bell Rings

(Life is like school, when the bell rings, we can all go home.)

Daily life goes on and on
Each day with all our tools
We come to learn and do our thing
Just like we are at school

To do what's right, to follow close
We have so much to learn
It's no wonder, to go home,
Is what we often yearn.

There is so much we don't know
A challenge to each day
So much to learn and absorb
Oh God help me that I pray.

The tests you give can be so hard
Sometimes they seem so long
I cannot find the answers here
The tests go on and on!

The bullies are so very mean
They push and scare away
We're frightened in these times of life
Struggling what to do or say.

Sometimes we're shunned by those around
Or others don't play fair,
Running through the halls of life
As of no one even cares.

This journey can be so hard at times
The day drags on and on!
I'm struggling so to just get through
How long will it prolong?

But then there times, a calming word
We read the Book you've given

Wandering Journey

The silent time of quiet prayer,
Gives us a taste of heaven.

A friend comes through, a teacher smiles,
And sometimes all play fair.
But then another test comes by
Or an obstacle we must bare.

The good news is the bell will ring
Will ring so loud and clear,
The day that Jesus does return,
The whole world will surely hear.

For when the bell rings, you will know,
It's homeward bound for you.
When Jesus calls, you'll know the time
As our world will end here too.

And joyously we'll run from school
To our heavenly home above,
A perfect world we will join,
Of peace, of hope, of love.

Desperate

It seems we do not realize
Just what we really need,
Until we become just desperate
Pleading from our troubles freed.

It is when we fall down on our knees
Because we are in such pain,
The misery we cannot stand,
Like pelting icy rain.

We finally let go of all our toys,
And hang-ups that we keep,
Let down the walls built up so tall,
We let go, and now we weep.

It is when we truly let it go
And let God in our life,
That we find a way, the better one,
That delivers us from strife.

Why did we wait for all those years?
Our pride got in the way
We hit our head against the wall
Our sins, we tried to pay.

So if you are trying to live your life,
Relying on your strength and power.
You will not make it, you will fail
Falling like a lifeless, dying flower.

The solution is a simple one,
Sometimes so hard to do,
Forget the pride; just take God's hand,
It is the best thing you'll ever do.

Some People See

It really is amazing; just what some people see
It all depends on perspective; what your vision is to be.

Some will see a derelict; on the curb of the street,
Others see a human soul, who's hungry with bare feet.

Some see morning as a time to hurry and beat the rush,
Others take a quiet time to talk to God in hush.

Some see elderly, just so old! So slow upon their feet!
Others see the faith and wisdom, as they sit with them to meet!

Some see a wait, a traffic jam! Irritating! It slows you down!
Others see chances to pray, to think about the crown.

Some see churches as hypocrites! They try to act so pure!
Others see a place for sinners, where sin can find a cure.

Some see the alcoholic as a waste; as worthless as can be!
Others see a traveled heart; longing to be set free.

Some see the dollar, so very great; number one thing in their life!
Others see that loving it, will defiantly cause strife!

You see, it's all perspective; the same thing that we see!
It's just what's in our heart and mind! Of what the image will be!

So if you see the empty cup; instead of what's half full!
You need to find a new source in life! That gives the right pull

That source is God; His son; the Spirit, they make three.
Pray to see with opened eyes; of what the "image" is to be!

To see the world in a new light, and find the work to do!
You'll see a change; a new look; with the eyes you're looking through!

When It Hurts

We get up every morning, walking in the same style,
Ways of self destruction, as we go from mile to mile.

Old habits and styles of living, destructive as they may be,
We keep on repeating, not listening, to the warning that we see.

We don't realize were trapped, in an addiction as a way
That leads to self destruction, no matter what others say.

The human way of thinking, "I know what's best for ME!"
"I want to do this my way, be quiet, let me be!"

We keep clinging to the stronghold that has robbed life today
Not thinking of it hurting others, or what price we will pay.

Then our world crashes, all around caves in
We're sitting on the bottom, wondering where we have been.

We do not like the gutter, the pain and misery here!
Why didn't I listen to others, who cared and shed the tears?

The mistake we made was not listening, until we felt the pain.
We marched on our way, and found nothing we'd gain.

It all could be prevented, if we'd let the Spirit in
To work with us and guide us, delivering us from sin.

God gives such a Spirit, a free gift to you and me.
Let it penetrate through your pride, from the stronghold set free.

If you see a pattern or style of living that you live
That leads to destruction, with no benefit to give.

Don't wait to hit rock bottom, or the gutter, don't you see?
Ask for the Holy Spirit to enter, and to set you free.

We can see a new world, when our soul seeks above,
When we ask God to deliver us, and fill us with His love.

Don't wait another minute, or repeat another day!
Allow God's intervention; let the Spirit guide your way.

What Do I Pray?

Sometimes I really wonder, just what I ought to pray,
For just exactly what to ask, or when or what to say.

Do I pray for healing? To be free from sick or ill?
Or do I pray for simply strength, to make it over the hill?

Do I pray for peace, throughout the world today?
Or do I pray for guidance, for our leaders of this day?

Do I pray that people, are happy and problem free?
Or do I pray that they can cope, with what they live and see?

Do we pray for specific needs? That job, that test, or a raise?
Or do we just hang in there, praying for guidance through the maze?

Am I being greedy or spoiled when I want my way?
Or should for the way I want my life, get on my knees and pray?

How can I confuse this so, it complicates my mind.
Should prayer be hard to do or say? The right words so hard to find?

Do I have the wisdom or the knowledge to ask for needs?
And problems or trials that help me grow, should I ask of them to be freed?

How can I know what's best for me? Or others in the world around?
The child, the sick, the hurting too? My answer may not be sound.

So when I'm not sure just what to pray, I'll pray what Jesus said,
"Thy will be done" in my life and world, and by His Hand be led.

The Ultimate Gift
"For Anyone Who Has A Child"

Our children are so beautiful; we love and care so much
The wonder of a little child, to cuddle and to touch.

They toddle around so bravely, and soon begin to speak,
Learning about all the world, their little brain does seek.

They grow so very quickly, soon a teen before you know
So much to learn, so much to do, and always on the go.

We give them all that we can, a home and clothes to wear,
To teach them right from wrong, we try not to fight, and show them to share.

The world seems harsh and cold, we protect them all we can
To keep the bad stuff from their life, from the present and future span.

We want them to be first in class, to excel in all they do
We're proud, we smile and get puffed up, after all, their part of you.

But it seems we miss the biggest thing that is in a child's life
The answer to their every need, that guides through pain and strife.

Do we teach them about our God above and how to pray each day?
To read the Bible and trust in the Lord? To seek God in all we do and say?

Do we take them to the church of God? Do we show them how to kneel?
Do we set an example for the child? By actions and how we feel?

Do we place God first in our life and follow words He has given?
Explain that earth is a journey to, our ultimate home in heaven?

Do we teach them all about our Lord and pray with them each day?
To worship God and view His world, on all we do and say?

The ultimate gift you give your child, nothing else on earth compares,
Do it now, it's not too late; it's the best gift you'll ever share.

Our Choice

God did not create robots, that move about here and there,
He created us as humans, with a mind and soul to bear.
A conscience He has given to help and guide us through,
As what is right or wrong in life, in what we say and do.
We can make the wrong decision, and close God to our heart,
We can live a life without Him, keeping miles and miles apart.
But if we choose that lifestyle, a force soon comes around
A sly and cunning evil force, that doesn't make a sound.
To control your thoughts and attitudes, your habits and your ways,
To change your purpose on this earth, take control of your days.
So remember it's your choice, of who will be your king
The way you choose to live daily, demonstrates what the future *will* bring.
If you turn from God and ignore Him, tune out the Word and Book
The sly one is soon smiling, as he holds out his evil hook.
To trap you into sorrow, into pain, distraught, and defeat
As he slowly pulls you to his ways, as he's grabbing at your feet.
So daily make a decision, that God will be your king
His way, His light, the Spirit, in your heart will daily sing.
Read the book, pray often! Ask God to guide your ways,
Accept the gift of Jesus, whose life given now does pay
When you've made this decision, the Spirit joins with you
New goals, and ways of living, will guide and walk you through!
Don't forget what's vital, who is number One today!
Keep focused and connected, to God throughout each day.

Words For My Friend

You feel the walls crumbling, sometimes bit by bit.
The world is caving in on you, the puzzle just doesn't fit.

Your dreams they all seem shattered, your hope is now so weak,
The sun seems dull, you feel so tired, and the future seems so bleak.

The anger and the hurt are there, the pain is sharp and deep.
It's so hard to keep on going, you'd like to hide and sleep.

You wonder if there is any hope, what are in the future plans?
Oh God! Help me I'm struggling so, I need some help, your hand.

Lift me from the dark and pain; help me walk with you today,
Guide me in what I say and do, I need to know the way.

And as you take His hand, you'll see, the walls stop falling down.
Bit by bit they start to shape, and hope will come around.

No matter what we face in life, people, trials, and the pain.
Remember God has a plan for you, even though it all seems like rain.

So take each day, one by one, stay close to your Father above.
He'll hold you close, guide you through, you're blessed with God's holy love.

Peacefully Finding God's Peace

I try every morning, to get up and go in peace
To keep my thoughts on target, for the turmoil all to cease.

I get dressed and hurry out the door, a positive attitude I will try
But soon the chaos hits me hard, and I begin to sigh.

I'm tired, so tired, of all of this, the bad news keeps rolling in
Garbling my mind, confusing me, and leading me right to sin.

I try to keep my focus on, the pure and what is right
But this crazy world confuses all, what a crazy sight.

The bills, the problems daily come, my dreams all tumble down
My friends they hurt, and then hurt me too, it keeps me in such a frown.
Take me from this chaos now! I'm tired and don't want to fight.
Take my away, I'm ready to go, I see no light in sight.

But wait, that's not the master's plan, he has other plans for you.
Let's calm down and start again, he'll walk or carry you.

If you feel that God has left you high and hanging from a limb
The clouds so dark and rain so cold, the future so gloom and dim.

Slow down and breathe, get on your knees, pray for healing from above
Heal my hands of Jesus now; turn this chaos to peaceful love.

There is a plan just for you, let go and let God lead.
He loves you so, He is in control, and because of Jesus you are free.

You do not need to worry all day, or think it all depends on you,
As God has a plan, He is in charge, and cares and loves you too.

So take each day, a gift from God, and live them one by one,
Hold tight, hang on, God's at your side, and will be till it's done.

And then the day will then appear, that we join him up in heaven
By simply believing in Jesus Christ and using the gifts he has given.

Knocking On Heaven's Door

We come to God in so many ways,
In thoughts, in silence and prayers.
We bring to Him our burdens,
problems, concerns, and our cares.

We bring a long list of troubles.
There are so many in life that you see.
And then there is all that surround us
Concerns for others, for you and for me.

There are all of those inconveniences
The problems that complicate days.
They keep us frustrated and troubled
Constant things that get in our way.

But do you really think when you are praying?
Of just who you are talking to?
As we hurriedly run through our list,
As we have so many things we must do.

Do you think about whose door you're knocking?
What a powerful God that you seek?
Do you think of Jesus your Savior?
We should be humble and meek.

When we walk on ground that is holy
We should think of whose presence we are in.
And talking to God is not a checklist
To request, and then be sorry for sin.

To pray is to come to our Father.
Through the gracious gift of His son.
What an honor, a wonderful blessing
To ask forgiveness for the sins we have done.

On knees that know we are humbled
A heart that is yearning for grace
A mind wanting to think and be purer,
A soul reaching for a glimpse of His face.

And our gratitude for all we are given
And our blessings in our cup overflow
We are often drinking from the saucer
The blessings of life we do not sow.

So when you knock on the door to heaven
Asking God to come into your day.
Open your heart, your mind, and your soul
You are talking to God when you pray.

Bearing Fruit

There is a lot of discussion
About what is the true way.
Of just how we get to heaven
Is it by what we do or say?

We know we cannot earn our way
By the good things that we do
We must accept our Savior,
He is the gate we enter through.

But some say, "I'll do just that!"
"I accept Jesus as the way,"
And then go on, not doing much
Thinking that's all they have to say!

So instead of producing fruit
They stop and do not grow
They say that's all that's needed
There's no more they need to show.

But I think that when your truly saved
And ask Jesus in your heart.
You'll see a pattern soon emerge
Because of your new start.

A new way of life will come around
To love, to grow, and to share
To give to others, to walk the way
And soon the fruit will bear.

God gives us each our special gifts
To serve daily walking in His way
Our talents, strengths, and the gifts we share
How we care and how we pray.

The fruit we bear will differ so
As we stay connected to the vine.
As he has a plan for what we do
Seek His word, and you will find.

So tightly cling to living vine.
The lifeline Christ gives to each.
So you produce the fruit you should
You don't have far to reach.

And even though some will grow
A harvest that looks so small
Others a vineyard will soon appear
Of fruit so firm and tall.

Our job is not to judge the fruit
For quantity or grade
Just follow God and do His will
Through the path that Christ has laid.

You'll find that accepting Christ
As your Savior and the way
And God the Father, the Almighty
That this is what you'll pray.

For life to be a growing field
Of fruit that you can bear.
Each day you grow and serve the Lord.
In truth, in love, and care.

What In The World Are We Doing?

What in the world are we doing
On this earth, in this country today?
Some of the things are just frightening
I wonder what God has to say?

With issues and decisions we're making
About God and prayers in our schools,
Taking God's name from our children's pledge
Who then, in their heart will soon rule?

We take and take and give nothing
Back to our earth, to our home.
Using resources, water and power
Taking land where our wildlife once roamed.

Our ditches are filled with clutter,
Of trash from meals as we drive.
We waste water and food and think nothing
Of those who struggle to survive.

We pass laws to make it legal
To end a child's life before its birth
Not thinking that they're God's creation
They are alive, heart beating, and of worth.

New laws introduced daily
To honor marriages of same sex in our states.
Don't you remember Sodom and Gomorrah,
And how that all ended, the fate?

The T.V. and radio are constant
News and the programs they show,
Does anyone care, does anyone think
Of where all this media goes?
Into the minds of our children
To help from their wrong and their right
It's part of the growing up process
Oh, how we cloud up their sight.

Wandering Journey

Our priorities, our time, what we're doing
Is it spent on family, God's plan, or His way?
Accumulating things, and getting more wealth?
Or concerned, what will the neighbors say?

What in the world are we doing?
Who is leading us as we go our way?
Why do we tolerate all the things that we do?
Why don't we stand together and say?

We have rights! We are the people!
We care for our country and land!
We are part of this earth and existence!
Part of this God created span!

Yes! We want God in our country and lifestyle
We want God to help as we plan
Our laws and judicial decisions
Oh help us to hold onto your hand!

God your earth is so very awesome
Let us care for it and tend to its needs
To enjoy the beauty and carefully share
And what we reap, replace with new seeds.

Let us teach our children good morals
Let them know who you are and the way
To keep you the number one priority
As we serve and live through each day.

Sunday Morning

Sometimes as people we often search,
For a God who politely stays at church.

Stays there all week, and on Sunday's there
So we can go visit, looking great and so fair.

We're clean and looking nice, dressed up with a smile
Willingly singing and hear the Word for a while.

But as we exit and go on our way,
We don't invite God home, at the church please just stay.

Don't follow me home! Don't come home today
I'm not sure if you'll like what I do or say.

I'll be back next week, just wait here in the hall,
And if it gets real tough, I'll give you a call.

And then we go off, to live out our days
Doing what we want, and having our ways.

Not doing what He tells us, not obeying the Word
Not remembering from Sunday, the message we heard.

And we wonder why life isn't going so great
We don't grow or develop just live life and wait.

For great things to happen! We can do it our way,
I'm quite independent! I know what to say.

I can plan my own future, the road that I take,
After all I'm not stupid about the decisions I make.

But living a week without God by our side,
Is futile and sinful, because of our pride.

If we remember the Book, the verse with the line,
We are the branch, and Jesus is the vine.

Wandering Journey

We cannot make it; we can't go on our own.
God holds our future, our seeds have been sown.

So to do what is planned, what God holds in store,
We must keep Him with us, each day and evermore.

We must open our hearts, our soul, and our mind
Invite God in daily, for then we will find.

The peace and the love, the joy, and the way
That God has planned, we just need to pray.

Daily asking him to bless you, and to be your guide.
He'll stay with you daily; He won't leave your side.

So next time when you go to church, slow down by the door,
Take God's hand as your leaving, He will hold yours evermore.

Thought Patterns

They come and go so quickly
They travel through our minds.
They control our way of thinking
And the source is hard to find.

Some bring a smile or laugh
Some a grin upon your face,
Some bring a heavy heart
To a current time or place.

Some bring up the evil
Of all that does surround.
Some pull out the past,
And all the details found.

Once a pattern emerges,
It doesn't take long to start
A trend or way of thinking
That affects your life and heart.

If that thinking is destructive,
Then the thoughts begin to show
And in your life the pattern,
Will soon sprout and start to grow.

Then vines will soon entangle,
And choke out the joy of life,
Negative ways of thinking
Centering on pain and strife.

Those destructive thought patterns,
The evil one is all aglow,
To see what really happens
When his work begins to grow.

It turns into a cycle
A continuing pattern that repeats
Pulling you down a gutter
Bringing depression and defeat.

Wandering Journey

There is a way to stop it,
And turn it all around.
It begins with where it started
And where the hurt is found.

Decide who you want to rule your life
Ask Jesus to take control.
Remove yourself from those temptations
That seems to tug and pull.

Start with a new fresh attitude,
As God your King and Source.
Of all you have, and all you own
Let Him be your new force.

Pray and ask for guidance
Ask for your soul to cleanse,
To terminate the choking vines,
And for His power to send.

Tender shoots of mercy
And new buds of love to share
For a fertile new foundation,
For your mind and soul to wear.

As when your thoughts are centered
On the Father who is King
Jesus works in your heart and mind
And new growth in you will bring.

A positive way of thinking,
To let go and let God guide the way
Your roots can grow, you see the light
As Jesus your debt did pay.

So do it now and quickly,
Don't go another day or hour.
Let God be centered *in* your thoughts,
To be your source and power.

Strongholds

We all seem to have them,
A stronghold in our life
It can ruin or torment us
And cause pain and strife.

Some people say, "It's my problem!"
"It only hurts just me!"
But they forget all of the others
That surround life, you see.

An addiction or a habit,
Giving into temptations way,
It could be the devils stronghold
Careful, there's a debt to pay.

Do we forget that God Watches?
He is there with all you do.
He follows us wherever we go,
And Jesus is there too.

And what about those around you?
Your family and your friends?
Your secret won't last forever
What message will it send?

The devil's work is strongholds.
That's what he does for fun.
To snag you and drag you down
So that you cannot run.

He wants you at his level!
He wants a grip on you.
He wants to own you bit by bit,
In what you say and do.

He'll hide the signs of strongholds
Call them "fun," "rest," or "play"
A way to "let loose, relieve the stress"
Or "wind down from the day."

Wandering Journey

But if it separates you,
From loved ones or friends
Causes pain or hurt
Or an unwanted message sends!

If you find that there is shame,
Of guilt about it all,
It hurts your walk with God,
Or you feel about to fall.

Then it probably is a stronghold
The devil is trying to snare,
To entice, and trap you in it!
Oh, he is so unfair!

If this picture looks familiar
And you recognize the view
You may realize a stronghold
That's happening to you.

Ask God to help you quickly!
To pull loose of the devil's reins.
To free you and to guide you.
To help you use your brains.

To clearly think about it
To ponder and decide
That you want the freedom from it
And God be at your side.

Pray for the forgiveness
To strengthen then repeat
And ask for guidelines daily
That the Holy Spirit is sent.

God will be with you always,
Just knock upon the door.
He'll give you strength and courage
Like an eagle you will soar.

Searching

Isn't it funny how in life we spend time searching
Searching for happiness peering round the bend
We look for friends hoping to find
One who will like us, a relationship that binds.
We want to look good, blend in with the crowd
Look good in the mirror, feeling both good and proud.
We search for a mate, the perfect find
Who matches as a soul mate, *in* both body and mind.
We search for good health, try all kinds of things
To keep bodies looking good, for happiness it brings.
We want security in our financial plan,
So we can sit back admiring our investment span.
And then comes a time, we sit back and we look
Feeling something is missing, like the theme of the book.
We're really not happy, we feel so alone
Like we're searching for something, *yet still we* roam.
Our friends let us down, they're not always true
Leaving us feeling, deserted and blue
Our looks they are fading, the sizes increase
And it seems we cannot find any inner peace.
Our health that may falter, we don't even know
Where tomorrow may lead us, where life will go.
We think that we have the perfect soul mate
And find that they leave us, or are lost to some fate.
The money, the savings, may not stay the same
The market it crashes, the world economy is to blame.
So while we're searching, what did we find?
No real security; no future to bind.
We needed that something, that wasn't on earth
But wrapped in a promise, our Savior's birth.
We need our real Father, always loving and there.
Who forgives, who creates, and helps us to bear.

Wandering Journey

Those times in our life, so empty, so lost
We found the answer simple, Jesus paid the cost.
So all of our searching, for all that we've found
Really wasn't the answer, we had been chasing around.
We should have been looking for our God is so great.
Who loves us and cares, who wipes clean our slate.
Our Maker, Creator, our Father high above.
Who forgives and guides, heals and shows love.
The good news is it is not too late
There is no need to keep looking, you don't have to wait.
Simply get on your knees, and bow your head down
And pray and confess, your life can be found.
True happiness and assurance, true security for life
No matter what happens, whether joy or strife.
God always has been there, and Jesus too
We searched for the wrong things, but what could God do
He waits for us patiently waiting to send
An angel of mercy, a saving hand.
But we first must believe, opening the door for Him,
As He won't enter our life, until we ask Him in.

Are You Calling?

Father, are you calling?
What is it that you say?
What is it that you want from me?
That I need to do today.

Is there someone that I should love?
Or someone who needs care?
Is there someone with such burdens?
They need someone to share?

Is there something in my life
That I'm doing that's not right?
Something causing pain or sin
And troubled, tossing nights.

Is there something that I love too much,
And am putting before you?
Are my priorities all messed up?
Tell me God, just what to do.

Is there a talent I'm not using?
A gift I do not share?
A quiet dream I've not pursued
A challenge I've not dared?

Where are you leading me?
Why are you calling me?
I feel the tug and pull right now!
Help me now to see!

I keep looking over here and there
To search for and to find
Help me know just what it is
Let it clearly be in my mind!

Am I too complacent sitting?
Do I need to move right now?
Am I stagnant and not growing?
Oh, God please show me how.

Wandering Journey

Father, are you calling?
Let me do your will today,
May your Spirit fill my heart and mind
On what I do this day.

Please take this life and let me be
An instrument for you,
That on this journey I may walk
Where you have asked me to.

Guests

Do we ever think whose place it is
That we live in every day?
Do we ever think that we're a guest,
Because we're not required to pay?

Yes, we buy and sell and think it's ours
Property and land and trees
Lakes and ponds and wildlife too!
We buy, we grab, we seize!

We dump our waste or bury it
Put chemicals on our weeds,
We pollute the air we need to breathe.
The lakes and streams they feed.

We consume and take, and do we care
About the generations yet to come?
Our children and their children too
Will they suffer by what we've done?

We are only really guests on earth
For the time that we're passing through
God gives us a great place to live
And this is what we do!

Why don't we care, slow down, and think
Of what is caused by our selfish ways?
Be responsible for what we do while here
Caring about earth's future days.

As a child of God, the gift we have
This earth and all that it gives
Let's act like a guest, thanks be to God!
For this earth where we're blessed to live.

The Ripple

Our thoughts can be so very strange
Our logic just a little bent
When we think that actions in our life
Cause no waves or ripples sent.

We say "It's my life and I will do!"
"I'm not hurting anyone!"
But that's not true, not at all!
Effects show up once it's done.

You see we are not an island
And all of those around
Are affected yes, by what we do
Whether it is a smile or frown.

You cannot cheat or tell a lie
Without someone who will know
You cannot hate or criticize
The effects will surely show!

The love you share, the laugh or smile
The hug, grin, or time
The meal you share, the listening ear
Or a lent dollar or dime.

It all affects those in your life
Those you come in contact to.
How you react, and what you say,
How you think and what you do.

It could be your child, wife, or son
Your brother or your sister
The person who lives down the street,
Or at work, the Miss or Mister.

It could be the grandchild not yet born,
Or the generation yet to come
That will be affected by what you do.
Even after your life is done!

Wandering Journey

So we are each a ripple
That continues on forever
It's what we do and how we live
We cannot stop or sever.

So live your life in such a way
That God has planned for you.
Of sharing love and giving hope
Live like Jesus wants you to.

Because as you live, you realize
That what you do and say
Is a ripple that continues on
May I live right, dear God! I pray!

Purity

Why is purity so old fashioned?
Like it just went out of style.
That to remain pure in heart
Is acting juvenile.

That language that is used each day
On the T.V. and on the screen!
Yet we sit and watch, hearing the words
Even though, they're coarse and mean.

Everything it seems that is advertised
On promiscuity is centered.
Is that what we want on children's minds
To grow up with, to be mentored?

To remain pure for your wedding day
Is that such an oddity?
Why can't we have the right to live
As God wants us to be?

Why put a dollar sign
So everything has a price?
And flaunt the dirty laundry
Of anyone who has a vice!

What is wrong with purity?
Why can't it be the way?
We live, we talk, and we center life
As we live in this world today?

Another's Strings

There are many things we do in life
That depends on one another
We could not make it through the day
Without that friend or brother.

But then there's things we must in life
Do only on our own.
No one else can take that step
Where our seed is placed and sown.

We have to do it on our own
From our heart it has to come.
No one else can take our place
For the race that we're to run.

That's how it is with our Father God
It has to be "our things"
God will not accept a heart
That hangs on another's strings.

It's your knees that have to touch the floor
It's your sin you must repent.
Your thoughts and your decisions made
Determine how eternal life is spent.

Worship must come from you
As do thankfulness and praise.
Thankfulness for all that you're blessed with
It's your arms that must be raised.

To be God's child, and adopted soul
It's your heart that must be given.
The transformation is in your own life
And how to treat your brethren.

To receive the gracious gift of grace
Must be accepted by only you.
Only your heart can be washed and cleaned
And life changed by what you do.

So if you think another's prayers
Will save your soul or life
Remember it is not what others do
That prevents your eternal strife.
So my friend, if your not sure
Where your eternal life will be
It's up to you, accept the gift,
Christ gave to you and me.

The Source

We think that we're so brilliant, in all we make and design.
We search for bigger and better, and things that take less time.

We use our mind for making, all sorts of things to use.
Some can be so harmful, in our world we do abuse.

How often do we really think? The source from where it comes?
We have the latest technology, but for creating we are dumb.

It is beyond our thinking and perception, of how thoughts start in our mind.
How the earth stays tilted, and perfectly, the planets all align.

How the air we breathe daily keeps the balance of oxygen just right.
The trees bud in the springtime, the stars shine so bright at night.

What tells us to keep breathing? Our heart beats on each day.
Gravity keeps everything planted, and the ocean knows where to stay.

It really comes down to the basics, our God, the world He does control.
He created our beautiful planet, and gave us bodies and souls.

So the next time you look at a sunset, and feel the wind blow on your face.
See raindrops falling gently, remember, it's all given by God's grace.

A Prayer From A Sinner

God you know I'm searching
I just cannot get satisfied
I'm restless and I'm troubled
It seems I've tried and tried.

I seem to get a handle
And feel like I've got it right
And then something comes up today
And I lose my grip and sight.

I try to be your disciple
I want to walk the way!
I want to be a child of God
In what I do and say.

And then I get discouraged
Because I let you down
I hurt those around me that I love
Instead of smile, I frown.

And the evil that surrounds me
Is overwhelming, I cannot get air
Does anyone know what's happening?
In our world, does no one care?

I scurry around so busy!
Futile thoughts occupy my mind
Influenced by secular thinking
With that, what will I find?

I know that I'll not be satisfied
By my works and what I do
The only way that I'll find peace
Is coming face to face with you!

So please forgive the messes
That I make in life each day
Forgive me when I'm useless
When I don't know what to pray!

Wandering Journey

Cleanse me from the countless sins
Have mercy on my heart,
For God, I want to be your child
Forever, may I not part.

I know I don't deserve this
I cannot earn it by what I've done
This is a gift, the grace of God
That was given by your Son.

Hurting

Why do we try so hard sometimes?
To hide just how we feel
To avoid those issues in our life
In our soul, they are so real.

They are like skeletons in our closet
May go back o'er lost years
But we cover them and hide them
With the hope no one finds them, we fear.

We act is if they don't bother,
If we ignore, they'll go away.
But they don't, they stay and linger
Because of the weight, we pay.

We try to cover them with denial
Or drown them with food or drink.
But then we deal with addictions
And further down we sink.

We punish ourselves in many ways
Without knowing that we do
We don't deserve, we're not worthy
But we keep that secret too!

So it all leads to a cycle
So vicious the pain we bear
Because we haul around luggage
We're not meant to carry, but share.

So if you look at your life and think
That you may fit in this routine
Well here is news to brighten you
As you're about to change the scene!

Clean out that closet of cobwebs
Pull out the skeletons you see
And give them to God, let go of them!
You'll feel better! You'll be free!

Soon there's not sorrow
Or such a problem as once thought
And you find you're not alone at all
As the devil had taught.

Don't waste another day
Here is the plan, use it and go
Open your heart and soul to God
As He loves you, don't you know!

The Restlessness Of Thirst

We become so very restless
When we know we need a drink
We're parched, we're dry, and we're looking so
We feel like we'll fall or sink!

So we try to quench with different things
To satisfy our thirst right now!
We're restless and we're desperate
As we struggle to find out how.

But no matter what we try in life
It doesn't quench for long.
We're back to thirst, searching again
It seems it was all too wrong

It's because the yearn for what we thirst
Is not found here on this earth.
It is the water that we need for life
That will give us a new birth.

It is living water that we need
That will quench thirst and will provide
The answer, want, and everything
If we ask God to our side.

And some day when we leave this world
We'll come to the great well.
Of living water so plentiful
When God rings the golden bells.

So drink up the living water
That God gives to all who ask
The water is so free and pure
In His love, you'll surely bask.

Lighthouse

Just what kind of lighthouse
Do we portray each day we live
What kind of light do we provide?
Do we take or do we give?

Do we encourage those around us
When they're struggling through the day?
Or do we just sit and watch
Because we don't know what to say.

Do we lend a helping hand
When someone is a little short?
Or if they owe and cannot pay
Do we drag them into court?

Do we show compassion
When one needs a listening ear?
Or do we pat them and walk away
As we don't have time for tears.

Is the love you give for everyone
Or just for a selected few?
Who agrees with your line of thinking
And all the things you do?

Do we forgive those who have wronged?
Forgive and get on our way
Or do we carry grudge and hate
To make sure that they do pay.

Do we gloat with pride
Of the great things we have done?
Or do we credit the grace of God
For all that He has done?

Just what kind of light beams
Do you send to those around?
Is it powered by a prideful heart?
Or from the power of God is it found?

If you're not sure and do not know
Then get down and begin to pray
That you can be a lighthouse
That God will use each day.

No Harm

If I can go to bed at night
And know I've caused no harm
That I have not caused pain or strife
Or no one alarm.

If I can live each day I live
And avoid giving that look or glare
But smile or give a gentle nudge
And any encouragement I may share.

If I can talk with those around
And use the tone of voice
That doesn't hurt or irritate
That goodness is my choice.

If I can see with eyes that see
The needs that do surround
If I can give to help one out
And do it without a frown.

If I can hear with ears that hear
And listen to what others say.
If I see a face, and feel their hurt
Or help them through a day.

If I can touch someone today
Rather than avoid and cross the street
If I can with a helping hand,
Reach and help them to their feet.

If I can cause no one pain
By what I do or say
But somehow bring a bit of joy
Or help throughout the day.

Oh God! I pray please take this life
And cleanse it from the old.
Help me not to hurt or harm.
But hear what you have told.

Wandering Journey

If I can live each day that is left
And not hurt the ones I see
But by your Word and saving grace
May live a life "harm" free!

Contentment

Do we ever find contentment
In the lifestyle that we live?
Or do we just pace the floor
Thinking life has more to give.

We never seem quite satisfied
With our look or current style.
The job is not what it should be
Your friends don't make the mile.

The house seems smaller day by day
Not as cozy or as bright.
The furnishings seems old and worn
A dreary boring sight!

You expect more from so many
They seem to let you down.
People just want more and more
When they bother to come around.

It's times like these we need to sit
And think about the ways,
We should be happy with what we have
As we live through every day!

Contentment is the key to this
To find that in your life,
Being satisfied with what you're blessed
Not struggling for more with strife.

If one can wake up in the day
And be thankful for what you own
For the family that you have today
Who make a house a home.

Contentment allows that you may live
So that you can truly share
Now you can focus on what to give
And life seems much more fair.

When you're content you feel whole,
You have not envy or greed
Your open mind is now so clear
From turmoil, now you're freed.

Do not dwell on your neighbor's grass
It's the same color as yours, you see.
As God has blessed us each so well
So that our heart is free.

Contentment is a key to life.
With what you're given, do your best.
Care and love, do what you can
Be happy with what you've been blessed.

Be Where You Are!

It seems a little funny
How we're always waiting for
This or that to happen
As we search for more and more.

In the middle of the busy day
We think about rest that eve
We can't wait for company to come
Yet glad when they finally leave

We sit and talk to our child
But our mind wanders soon away
Thinking about things at work
Or monthly bills we have to pay.

We're sitting in the church pew
Singing worship and *using* time to pray
But we think about the neighbor
Sitting next to us today.

We don't take time to appreciate
Just what blessings we have right now
We don't live in our "present"
Because we don't know how!

We need to "be" where we are
No matter what it entails
Whether joy, or tears, or sorrow
Great success or failures.

If we don't experience what we live
We don't "feel" life as we go
We'll miss so much, *and* won't realize
What God's plan is for us to know!

It may be tears or happiness
It may be sickness too
It may be joy or quiet time
But it's all designed for you.

Wandering Journey

So as you live, "be there"
Experience each day and hour
God's given you this gift of life
It's from His hand, His power.

Short Term Living

We live as if we're limited
To a hundred years or less
Thinking it all stops at death
So now, we must get success!

We try not to think of afterlife
Or dwell on eternity
As we concentrate on trivial things
On what we hold and what we see.

This life here is just a starting point.
Our death, just a transition
And how we live and what we do
Determines our eternal position.

Our purpose here is not our needs
To get just our way and will!
God has a plan, a purpose for us
It's our choice, if we fulfill.

So if you're concentrating
On the short term way of life
Your eternal destination
May be filled with pain and strife!

Start thinking in the long term
When coming forth from our cocoon
We do not know the place or time
It may be long or soon.

But our life here is not final
When we die and leave this place
As we go to our new homeland
And see our Father's face.

So invest in your eternal
The long term life it does await
Live today for your tomorrow
So you enter through God's gates.

What If?

What if people loved people?
With compassion we held out our hand.
If hate and hurting stopped at this moment,
Kind acts would be as numerous as sand.

What if one world we united
To love, to care, and to share.
War and hatred were not present,
And world problems together we'd bear.

What if all people loved their children
And genuinely nurtured their young.
There was no abuse or abandonment
Only love from their heart would be sung.

What if we cared for God's creation?
The earth, the ocean, and the sky
We didn't pollute or destroy
But take care of this earth, we would try.

What if our research was founded?
On good and what's best for our soul
Not self-centered or even destructive,
That can carry such a big toll.

What if hunger was ended!
And the lost and forgotten were found.
Everyone tried to do their best
And we knew that our future was sound.

What if we found answers to living
From God's book, and sharing, and love?
Not booze, drugs, or other vices
But look to our Father above.

What if we all believed in one God?
And to him we'd cling to His side.
Wouldn't it be a bit of heaven?
In this world that we all abide.

Wandering Journey

What if today is the last day?
That you're given to live out your life.
Are you heavenly bound to go to our King?
Or are you heading for pain and for strife.

It's all about what you choose in life
You know the truth and the way.
What if Jesus came knocking?
At your heart and your doorstep today?

Boilermaker's Daughter

As I look back at younger days
Of memories as a child
Some days were calm, a little slow
Some more exciting, even wild.

But clear to me are memories
Of the lifestyle of my father.
And how I grew up in my life
As a boilermaker's daughter.

Dad's trips were long, miles away
Sometimes for weeks and weeks.
Overtime and seven twelve's,
At those checks, we'd like to peek!

Sunday eves were often sad
When he'd have to hit the road.
A cooler full of lunches made,
A standard to be towed.

With love beads hanging on the mirror
His cap in the backseat,
A suitcase full of blue jean clothes
And work boots for his feet.

But always happy was the day
When Dad rolled into town!
We'd hug, laugh, and horse around
There never was a frown!

We'd hear about guys on the job
Dad's crazy jokes and stories,
Welding in the heat of day,
Driving home through blinding flurries.

And through it all, what I know and learned
Was Dad's love and how he cared.
We did not know the trials he had
And all the troubles bared.

Wandering Journey

Through it all, we always had
Everything a child could need.
By our Dad, who loved us so
By words said, and his kind deeds.

God watched over him, I am sure
Through the travel and the days.
To keep him safe, on the right track
Dad has always known the way.

God, thank you for these memories
Thank you so much for my father
I am blessed and thankful so
To be a boilermaker's daughter.

Trivial Pursuit

I think as I live and learn
There's something I begin to see
That becomes clearer as I live
To make a change in me.

We pursue so much that trivial
It doesn't matter much at all.
We hoard, we buy, and we get big plaques
And put them on our walls.

We talk about who's doing what
And who's in the news today.
How much and where we spend our cash
And is that too much to pay?

It all seems just so trivial
When you open and read God's book
As to what is really important
In our hearts and mind to look.

We pursue what rusts and rots
And those who walk away.
We pursue what looks so pretty,
But fades the next day.

Our trivial pursuit of living
Our Father shakes His head
When will they see or learn?
In the Book, it's all been said.

Our pursuit of what is important
Comes down to basic things
Our relationships and how we love
Our soul and what it sings.

We can't take belongings with us
When we die and leave this earth
We'll have the same amount of things
That we did the day of birth.

Wandering Journey

So before you go on chasing
All those things you yearn to own.
Think about where your heart is
And how much in life you've grown.

Are you loving all that you can love
Giving all you can give?
Sharing all you can share
Are you happy with how you live?

Just what are you pursuing?
What's on your heart today?
If you're not sure, just ask God.
He'll lead you as you pray.

Forgiven

To know that I'm forgiven
What a blessing and a gift
To take the burden and the guilt
And from my soul do lift.

To cleanse me from the muck and mire
And filth that I acquire
And clean me white as snow dear God
What more could I desire?

The time I took your name in vain
The time I turned my head
The time I shuddered about what I did
And words that I had said.

When I didn't' seem to care at all
About my body or mind
When instead of you I searched
For happiness that I couldn't find.

When I did not even take the time
To thank you or appreciate
When I felt what happened in my life
Was all left up to fate.

When I felt I could not say no
To temptation or to sin
When habits or addictions pulled
And I simply just gave in.

When I let anxieties make me sick
And keep me up all night
When I did not trust or come to you
But trembled with fear or fright.

My God I confess them all to you
And lay them out for you to see
And I thank you God that Jesus took
All these sins away from me!

Wandering Journey

So as I live each day by day
And go to bed at night
I have the comfort that I'm saved
And God will hold me tight.

All because of God's great gift
And Jesus and the tree
My sins are washed, my past is clean
And now my heart is free.

The Prodigal

I come to you, I cannot look up
My heart, my soul feels dead.
I've hurt and sinned, I've messed up so
And can hardly lift up my head.

The sins are all so heavy
A fool, yes that was me.
I frittered away all my gifts
I was so blind, I just did not see.

The beauty of the innocence
Is gone, and now down the drain
The energy of life is all faded
All that's left is this awful pain.

I deserve to be rejected
And yet here I am crawling back to you.
With tear stains on a dirty face,
I just did not know what else to do.

And then I feel a heavenly touch
A hand that's filled with love.
I feel the embrace of forgiveness
From the One who is above.

I cry, I do not deserve this!
I feel so bad about what I've done
Yet, I'm accepted, I am forgiven
I'm a daughter, and I am a son.

I cannot utter a single word.
No words there are to explain
This gratitude and grace given
This end to all of my pain.

I rebelled against everything
I ran and went totally wild
And now here I am, taken back.
You're my Father, and I am your child.

Wandering Journey

Oh, thank you so, for this moment
For this hand that now touches me
I pray that somehow through your grace and love
I'll be the child, which I was meant to be

The Prodigal's Elder

The elder looks upon them, watching "the Father and the son"
The youngest is gently sobbing, for all the things he's done.

The Father holds the youngest closely, as he forgives and he accepts
Loves the son unconditionally, has cancelled all his debts.

The elder thinks and wonders, of all the days and years
He's been true to the Father, through laughter and through tears.

And now they throw this party, inviting all to come,
As if it's all forgotten, they celebrate and just have fun.

The elder reflects how daily, did obligations he knew he should,
Always and reliable, because the Father knew he would.

The elder thinks, "This is not right" there is no fatted calf for me,
No robe, or ring upon my hand, this really should not be.

The Father calls, to the eldest, "Come on along, you are my son,"
"All I have is yours you know, your welcome, please do come."

The elder stands with fists clenched tight, he cannot move at all,
Cannot forgive, resents it all, he stands proud and he stands tall.

Do you ever see a little, of the elder in you and me?
Do you ever see a hardened heart; one will not allow to be free?

No one appreciates you at all! Your work, your sweat, and your time.
Even though it wasn't in your heart, you did it all just fine.

Does a little of the elder, exist somewhere within us all?
Do we try to analyze too much? And find we miss our call.

Our Father, He does love us, each unique and unconditional,
We need only open our heart to him; his love can fill us full.

The Father, He is calling, the celebration will soon begin,
With open arms and loving grace, you need only let Him in.

Global Warming

We hear of global warming
How it will change the earth
Of how it is now spreading
To affect our life and worth.

But what about another kind
Of global warming that could be
The warming of the heart of man
The change that all could see.

The warming of cold and empty hearts
The Word of God for all
The warming of apathetic air
By responding to God's call.

The warming of hate and blame
That changes to love and understanding
The warming of the need of greed
Instead of a helping hand.

The warming of a cold dark sin
To forgiveness with a smile
The warming of a worn out soul
With a friend who walks the mile.

The warming of cold and bitterness
Instead, one learns to grow.
The warming of self centeredness
To concern, that really shows.

This will happen upon this earth
A warming of the heart of man
And make a difference, you will see
As it is all in our Father's plan.

Amen.

Looking Over Your Shoulder

The tattered poor old women
Drops two coins into the plate
She gives it all, she doesn't skimp
For more savings, does not wait.

She is not walking proudly
To make sure that all can see.
But goes meekly and mildly
Unnoticed by you and me.

Have you ever done a kind act?
Spent time with poor or broke?
But while you're reaching out you hand
With your other, expect a stroke?

Do we work for a collection
Of the grand things that we do
To put upon display for all
To frequent and look through.

Or do we give with one hand
The other does not know
Do we love, bless, and share it
From us does giving flow.

In such a way, it is not seen
Quietly, it is not heard
With love and care, we share it all
And may not say a word.

As when you act in ways of God
To serve and do His will
It's not the attention that you want
But His plan, for you to fulfill.

Remember the poor old women
Remember the coins she gives
Don't look for others attention
That's how God wants you to give.

The Last Time

We never know when it will be
The last chance we have on earth
To give a smile or parting word
To show someone their worth

We never know what day will be
The last someone will live
Nor do we know the time we have
To share, to love, to give

So don't hold back a hug or smile
Don't put off another day
Take the time you have right know
In what you do and say

There may not be another chance
In their life to share that word
It may be the last opportunity
For your voice, to them, be heard

So stop and give that extra hug
And encouraging word or smile
Tell someone you love them too
Or help them with a trial

Our days they have a limit
Today may be the last
And the people you encounter
May soon be in your past

The next time that you see them
May be in heaven above
And they come up and tell you thanks
For your earthly share of love

Turning The Other Cheek

Jesus told us long ago
The other cheek to turn
But it can be so very hard
So very hard to learn.

When wronged and not treated right
When someone takes from you
Do we have to turn the other cheek?
Isn't there something we should do?

Is that what Jesus said to us
To be weak, or to look small
When someone trips us up today
Do we stumble, do we fall?

Or is it the condition of your heart
How we react and what we say
Do we forgive and move ahead
Or let it ruin our day?

Do we let revenge rule our mind?
Getting even our major plan
Or consider the shoes of which they walk
Try going on the path they ran.

I do not have the answers
Just what did Jesus mean?
But I trust God to help me see
On Jesus' words, I lean.

So help me when I want to fight
When my first thought is getting even
That I may see things differently
I may think that I may reason.

That I may possess discernment
Of what it is that I should do
Being able to turn the other cheek
When Jesus wants me to.

In The Blink of An Eye

We act like it will not happen
We think it's far away
But we do not know the place or time
Will it be night or day?

We take each day for granted
And act like we have time
To get it all together
For our salvation we will find.

We procrastinate because we're busy
With the fuss of all around
When it all may end in a moment
Just where will our heart be found

In just the blink of an eye
It may be our last breath on earth
And then it will change all that is
Just like the time of birth.

It tells us in the Bible
It is no secret for you and me
It is clearly written, yes it will happen
And you'll have no time to flee.

So think about each day you live
Each minute, just what you do
What is the condition of your heart?
And where does your final home lead you to

We do not know the day or time
We need to be prepared
And know our God and saving grace
And how our Jesus shared.

Don't take another minute
Without getting your heart right
Accept God now and forever
Let Jesus wash you white

Wandering Journey

As in just the blink of an eye
This earthly life will cease
And you want your final destination
To be full of love, joy, and peace.

Putting It All Together

Why do we make compartments
For aspects of our life
A place for friends and family
For husband and for wife.

Then in a separate place
We put work or our career
And build up walls between each
With hopes, dreams, and fears.

Our spiritual life, we keep separate
Reserved for certain days
For places in which we worship
As if it's just a phase.

Is it wrong to be a family man
When you work throughout the day
Can you achieve the goals you have
While walking in God's way.

And what about being a Christian
Faith in our God above
Is it a part of our daily stride
Our decisions, how we love

We each have just one heart
One mind and soul we bear
Why do we try to separate
Parts of our life, we care

God can make us whole again
Our roles in life entwine
And put it all together
God's plan for us we find

God made us as one person
He made us whole and driven
To do his will throughout our life
When it ends, to be in heaven.

Wandering Journey

Take down the walls that separate
God fills the gaps with his grace
So you may shine in all you do
And in the end, you'll see God's face.

When Christ Is In Your Heart

When Christ is in your heart
You know there is a change
When a confrontation happens
You cannot go estranged.

A voice may talk so softly
Or yell into your ear
You cannot sleep or rest at all
Or look into a mirror.

Until you have made right
The wrong that you must face
And reconcile and get on track
The source, you must trace

You'll have to swallow pride
And sometimes compromise
Because of love's great power
You repair the broken ties.

When Christ lives in your heart
You change priorities
To do His will and walk the path
From sin you want to flee

And when you mess it all up
And know that you have wronged
You must confess and reconcile
You don't want this to go on.

Christ stirs you heart and comfort zone
Can make you so aware
When you are not following His way
You'll confess to Him and share.

You know that Christ is present
Your heart He penetrates
Abide in Him and walk the path
That leads to our final gate.

Wandering Journey

We know this is a journey
A time to learn and grow
So when He speaks do listen
And your "Christlikeness" will show.

The Warmth of the Son

It is so cold and very dark
There is frost on everything
The sun peaks onto the sky
And warming rays does bring.

The frost soon melts quickly
The cold now fades away
The earth is warmed by the sun
And begins a bright new day.

The warmth of the sun does penetrate
Through the darkness of the night
To bring the rays of sunshine
And provide us glorious light.

God also gives another Son
To warm the coldest heart
To change a dark life in light
And give us a new start.

The Son of God, He came for us
And lives with us each day
Warms our heat, soul and mind
The Spirit for us prays.

The light He brings helps us to see
Our life in a different glow
So we may bear fruit and do His will
From us, love and care will flow.

Our God, He is so kind and good
For our earth the sun He gives
But the Son of God, He died for us
And arose, so we may live.

Eternity

Why do we try to separate
Our life while here on earth
As if eternal does not come
Until after death, there is no birth.

For what and how we live our life
What we believe and do
Determines what and where we'll be
The gate we enter through.

We each have a destination
One determined by our heart
We can accept or reject Jesus Christ
It's our choice, He did His part.

It's all a part of a journey
Our soul, God did create
We are all made eternal
Our choices determine life or fate.

So do not limit living
While here on earth each day we live
As it is all part of a spectrum
We can take or we can give.

And we never know the moment
When the gate of death will come
And the rest of life will either be
In the dark or in the "Son"

Each day and every moment
It matters how we live
What we say and what we do
How we share and how we give.

When God made us in His image
Our soul created from above
We are made to be eternal
Praising God and giving love.

You Can Always Look Up

When the world is all around you
And you feel you cannot breathe
Someone is pushing in behind you
And in front, they will not leave.

The pressure builds, you can't get air
It gets tighter as you go
You try to walk the path you should
But the load is too hard too low.

It seems no one will stop to help
They do not see or hear
You're anxious and distraught inside
There is only stress and fear.

Remember that you're not alone
When you think there's no way out
You need only look up to the sky
As there is another route

As when you call and seek our God
He never leaves your side
There's always hope and light above
His love for you abides.

Just seek him and soon you'll find
The pressure will go down
And all of those who locked you in
Have left, they're not around.

Because our God provides us air
That calms our heart and mind
He sends us light, a ray of hope
The tension now unwinds.

So do not forget to look up high
As there is always light to see
God always is there to guide and love
He cares, He'll set you free.

Surrender

I need to do the hardest thing
I have ever done in life
More than all the suffering
I've dealt with pain and strife.

I need to let go of selfish desires
Let go of worldly ways
Let go of goals that seem to be
Part of this earthly craze.

I need to let go of my fears
Of life and death and pain
Of loneliness and sickness too
The cloud of pouring rain.

I need to let go of my pride
The need to have my way
The need to have it always be
Just what I plan or say.

I need to see through different eyes
That my purpose is not complete
That I may not know just what it is
I'm not in the driver's seat.

I need to surrender all to God
My heart, my soul, my mind
I need to let Him lead me on
With no fear of what I find.

Let God take control of it all
And take the plunge for good
And not turn back, but dive right in
I knew before I should.

So God, I'm here with open heart
Empower me with your Spirit today
May I live my life with you in control
You are my Potter, I'm the clay!

Grace

When we share God's grace with others
It may require some time
It might be an inconvenience
It may put you in a bind.

That phone call that takes longer
Because someone needs to talk
The extra time that it takes
To help someone along, to walk.

The effort to go across the room
Or maybe across the street
To share a meal or helpful hand
To help someone you meet.

To write that note or send a card
Or give your coat away
To teach someone or help them out
Adds sunshine to a day

By the wondrous gift God gives us
Of grace, so abundantly it flows
Share the grace that you are given
So the Grace of God can show.

Redemption

We often wonder how something good
Can ever come from bad
How any kind of joy at all
Can result from things so sad.

What possibly can come from things
That stress us so in life?
How can we ever grow or learn
From all this pain and strife.

But yet it does, if you look
At the picture as a whole
Not just at a time or place
But let the tapestry unroll.

If you're not sure ask Moses
Or the woman at the well
Ask Peter or ask the Samaritan
Of stories they could tell.

Somehow our God redeems it
With a power and a plan
To turn things all around and then
Make them precious with His hand.

The pain we sometimes suffer
The hurt that we go through
When later we look back and see
We matured and learned, we grew.

So when it all seems futile
And you cannot walk the mile
Remember God redeems us
And that may bring a smile

Because we're all in this together
There is a plan here to unfold.
And God is in the center
As in His hands He holds.

The answers to these questions
The love and strength we need
God can and will redeem us
You can count on Him indeed!

Just Because

Just because I'm a Christian
Does not mean I'll never sin
That I'll not have a bad day
I can lose, not always win.

Just because I'm a Christian
I'm still human on this place
I'll mess up and need forgiveness
I'll have dirt upon my face.

It's because I am a Christian
The blessings I receive
Are from a forgiving, loving God
When I'm in sin up to my knees.

Because I am a Christian
I know there's a hope for me
Jesus loves and forgives me
From my awful sins, I'm free.

Because I am a Christian
I grow closer to God each day
Bear fruit as Jesus prunes me
For neighbors, I care and pray.

God transcends all understanding
His power, His grace, and His ways
Because I am a Christian
I can live on earth today.

To Turn Or Shake

Sometimes I get confused
And don't know what to do
Do I turn the other cheek
Or shake the dust off of my shoe.

When people treat you badly
And you've tried and tried again
To make amends or share a word
But they won't oblige or bend.

When they lie, cheat, and hurt you
And promises do not keep
Should you respond and get mad
Or just sit down and weep.

Do I turn the other cheek
When I just can't take no more
Or simply shake the dust from my feet
And just walk out the door.

Jesus tells in the Book
The other cheek to turn
Yet on another day and time
Two walk away and not to yearn.

I pray and pray about it
Yet do not know what is right
When I'm hurt, tired, and confused
I need guidance and some light.

So Jesus help me through this
Let the Spirit work in me
And whatever way you lead me to
I'll go, just help me see.

I trust in you Lord Jesus
I trust the words you say
I know you'll help me Jesus
As I face these things today.

Wandering Journey

From this I hope to grow and learn
May I walk closer than before
I want to do your will, oh God
Tell me to turn, or walk out the door.

Ignoring God

It doesn't even sound right
To ignore our God, we say,
But it happens oh, so frequently
Almost every day.

We get busy with our earthly stuff
And are so preoccupied
That we don't take time for God at all,
And shrug, and say, "I tried!"

The Bible gets so dusty
Our prayer life is so lean
Thanksgiving and our praise to God
Is seldom ever seen.

We drive by autumn forests,
And rainbows in the sky
Not noticing God's great gifts,
As we hurry, and rush by.

The talents that we're given
To serve and fulfill God's way
Are often never blossomed
In a cocoon, they simply *stay*.

We indulge and occupy our mind
With futile races here each day.
Running here and running there
Hardly thinking what we say.

How can we ignore our God?
How can we tune Him out?
God is the center of our life
He is what it's all about.

So think about the time you spend
And what you do each day you live.
Think about what's on your mind
On what, in life you give.

Wandering Journey

And if God's not on your "To Do List"
If you have not thanked God today
If your talents are not blossoming
And you have not stopped to pray.

Maybe you need to check your heart
Your soul and road you're on.
Maybe you need to change your plans
And sing a brand new song.

Everything that is in your life
Everyone you love so dear
Every minute of each day
Is a gift from God, right there.

So if you think you've no time for God
Quick, change your priorities
Because God is the only way
For today and eternity.

Lukewarm

In this day and present age
It is easier don't you know
To stay right in the middle
And just go with the flow.

By avoiding some commitments
Or an obligation we can defer
Then we don't make much of a wave
Rather find a convenient detour.

We sort of stay just lukewarm
Not hot, or cold, just in between
Because it just is easier
We blend in and we're not seen.

Sometimes we can get by with this
We sort of just float on by
And don't get too excited
Rather sit back, relax, and sigh.

But this does not work with our faith
Jesus explained that to us all
We cannot be just lukewarm
When we answer to God's call.

You can't be half committed
You can't have faith just half the time
You have to dive right in there
And trust God all the time.

You can't be half a Christian
You can't sit back watching your life go by.
You have to stand up for what is right
You have to move, to try!

You have to give your entire heart
Your soul, your thoughts, your mind
You have to open up to God
Like a book, so He can find.

The bread that Jesus offers
When He offers, you must take
You must then take the plunge of life
You must eat, you must partake.

You can't be a lukewarm Christian
God wants your heart, your soul, your mind.
Just take the bread, and eat it now
And to Our God, forever bind.

In It Not Of It

We have no other choice
But to live in the world each day
We must survive and interact
And yet find time to pray.

You have to make a living
And send your kids to school
Yet try to live and be a friend
Follow the golden rule

The world sneaks right in your home
The news, the mail, and such
You try to live simple and pure
With a caring hand do touch

The race in on, forward we go
Possessions, power, and pride
Or have we shared what we have
Then find someone has lied.

Why do we have to deal with
The hate, the pain, the greed
The lust, the hurt, and the selfishness
From this can't we be freed?

But God created each of us
He gave us each free will
Some then will follow him
Others selfish needs fulfill

We must live here in this world
But we do not have to be
Part of the world that is not right
A choice for you and me.

Help me not be of the world
To fall in the traps and snares
But closely stay to you my God
To the hand I know that cares

Wandering Journey

And because of you Father God
Because of Christ your son
I know I can face the road ahead
Till my earthly road is done

My eyes are set on heavenly gates
Where there is no pain or strife
Where all is good and at peace
Where we are with you the rest of life.

The Crutch

Some think they really need them
In life, they can't go on
Without the crutch to help them
They will not get along.

The crutch can be a person
The crutch can be a thing
The crutch may be drink or drug
Or money, and what it brings.

The crutch can make you stumble
The crutch can make you fall
You can't stand up without it
Even then, you're not so tall.

You are not independent
You need others to get by
You find ways and make excuses
Or hide, or may get high.

When Jesus walked upon this earth
And reached out to the lame
He did not give out crutches
He healed them, poor and maimed.

And that is what God does for us
When for help we call to Him
He gives sufficient grace and love
He gives us strength within.

So don't call out for crutches
To Jesus you must go
He will heal you in your heart
And God's love will show.

Don't think that you are disabled
The crutch just thrown away
And be a child of the Holy God
He will help you walk today.

Our Mission

Do you think you have no mission?
No purpose to exist
And if you had to name it
There would not be a thing you could list

Well if you're struggling down this path
Here is a word or two for you
Because there is a plan in life
Of what God wants you to do!

God created you just like you are
You're unique, one of a kind
Your soul and all you do and say
And what is on your mind

You have been blessed with talents
Of which you may not realize
But they are there, clear as can be
Right before God's eyes

God put us here to love Him
He put us here to share
He put us here to laugh and cry
He put us here to care.

He wants us to share the Word
To share His grace and power
To be a vessel of His love
From a seed, become a flower.

So we can share the beauty
A fragrance oh so sweet
To bear fruit from the flower
And lay down at His feet

And then the heavenly promise
Of eternal life a gift for all
Simply by belief in God
For old, and young and small.

Wandering Journey

If you don't know what you're doing
Or where you're going today
There is a mission for your life
Just ask God, to find the way.

To share what He has blessed you
To fulfill His master plan
To touch a heart, or save a soul
To love God all that you can.

Expectations

As we relate to those around us
Our family and our friends
Our soul mate or our spouse
With whom our life we spend.

We all have expectations
From those people whom we relate
Expectations that are planted
Of the child, or friend or mate.

Sometimes we think they'll fill a gap
Or hole that's in our heart
We trust in them to help us out
Or gives us a new start!

Some expectations are so little
Some impossible to attain
No matter how someone tries
Through tears, or trials, or rain.

And then we feel abandoned
Or abused or even lost
Because they failed and let us down
They did not know the cost.

So we blame it all on the others
We failed what we anticipate
We search and look for someone
Who won't lead us to such fate.

But when you live with humans
Like we all do as we live
None of us are perfect
No matter how much we give.

We can't always fulfill another
We can't meet that every need
We try and try, it doesn't work
And seldom do we succeed.

Wandering Journey

There is only one in the creation
Of the whole existence, don't you see?
Only one who is truly perfect
Exceeding all the boundaries.

Only God will fill the gap
Only God is there each day
Only God will love and care
Knows our needs before we pray.

So put your expectations
On the Rock who wears the crown
On Jesus Christ our savior
God never lets us down!

Sovereignty

How could God let this happen?
Did He turn His back on me?
Even when I tried so hard
If He was here, I did not see!

Why did things have to go this way?
Did this, I just deserve?
Even when I tried so hard
To listen, and to serve.

Why was I left all alone?
Where was God when I needed Him most?
Where was divine intervention?
Where were the heavenly hosts?

And so many go on living
Without a problem it seems, or a trial
Just having it all fall into place
Try walking in my shoes a mile.

And then I start thinking
What right do I have to say
To question, complain or to fret
About what I experience each day.

Our God, He is sovereign
There is nothing that happens here
That God has not first filtered
Whether it be smiles or tears.

No, we don't have all the answers
And if we could, we would not understand
Because God is our God Almighty
And our life is all in His hands.

Every particle in this universe
Every soul, every mind, every heart
Every moment of time and each century
Of His plan, we are all a part.

Wandering Journey

But yet God gives us free will
We can thank Him, or we can complain
We can share and love, or hate and hurt
Bask in sunshine, or crawl in the rain.

Our God, oh yes, He is sovereign,
And if we choose in faith that we live
We will always know He is with us
All the love that He has to give.

So I'll not dwell on the questions
All the answers, I cannot find
But humbly, I'll go to my Father
To His love, I want to bind.

Someday, it may seem much clearer
When we die and leave this place
But for now, I'll trust in my God
I'll hold His hand, and look to His face

Look out on the whole universe
At the life and how history spans
It's all from a sovereign God
A God, it's all in His hands.

Two Lives

Sometimes I feel I live two lives
I go back and forth each day
In what I'm focused on in my life
And what I do and say

I read the Bible and pray each day
To come close to God in life.
Then get dressed and out the door
Facing a world of struggles and strife.

I try to keep thoughts on heaven
And look to my Father above
To pray for those who surround me
To act kindly, share and love.

But when you go out into this world
That we live and encounter each day!
It's so hard to try to stay on track
On the things earlier I prayed.

The news can be depressing
The world keeps you anxious and stressed
Your hope fades, your smile frowns,
And it's hard to do your best.

The quiet moments of peace that I had
Are interrupted by those around
You don't know why people do what they do
Where on earth can sanity be found?

As the center of all is money
And all that it brings we buy
To get what we want, it doesn't matter
On whom we will hurt as we try.

I want to stay focused, keep going!
Keep my eyes and heart doing what's right
For some peace, and some kind of contentment,
When I lay down my head at night.

Wandering Journey

So here I am pleading again Lord!
To stay connected to you as I go.
The world pulls and tugs, and makes it hard!
Oh! I need some help! Please show.

But now, I think that I'm seeing
The message that I am to see
I'm part of this world, not separate
So maybe there is hope for me

If I can shine even just a little
In this life in something I do
To bring God's light to this world
As each day that I live passing through.

Somehow I have to be able
Stay connected to God all day!
And bring His power and mercy
To others by what I'm doing today.

So please let my light shine for you Father!
May I bring light to this world in some way
Please guide me and give me direction
Of your bright light, may I be a ray.

Wondering

Have you ever wondered where God came from?
And just how He made it all?
How could He make the earth so grand
And delicate things so small?

Have you ever wondered how it works?
How God knows each of us on earth?
How He hears the prayers that we say
And knows us before birth.

Have you ever wondered if God was near?
Was He there when times were tough?
Or did He leave and let us fall
When things were going rough.

Have you ever wondered how God speaks?
And why He sometimes seems still?
When we seek and ask and plead for help
And are praying for His will.

Have you ever fallen on you knees
And cried, face wet with tears?
And wondered where we go in life
As we look back at passing years.

If you too, have struggled my friend
And questioned or wondered why
If you have stumbled through the day
That ends the night with sighs

Well there is a God, He hears our prayers
He made the large and the small
He knows our heart and what we think
Our problems, struggles, and falls

He knows they day we were born
The trials and troubles we bear
He knows the joy, and the fun we have
And all who we love and care.

Wandering Journey

So if doubt is clouding your mind today
Your confused and don't know the way
Let me tell you some things that I do
That may help your journey today.

Just keep your faith and keep going
Talk to God in your thoughts and prayers
Keep going to church, and do what's right
Because your heavenly Father cares.

And when you don't know the answer
Remember that God does above
And that's the way that we'll go through life
Because of our Father who loves.

Pity Parties

We throw such big parties
And ask for all to come
To hear about our problems
Asking when will they be done.

We can't break that lousy habit
Self control we don't possess
It's all the fault of someone else
Not fair we lack success.

We work hard ever minute
With no gratitude or thanks
And never get promoted
Stay stagnant in the ranks.

No one seems nice or caring
Sometimes people seem so foul
Never smile or nod their head
Just a glare or a mean scowl.

All that happens in your daily walk
Is bad, it is just not fair
Black clouds just seem to linger
Seem with no one else they share.

No one else has these problems
We really cannot bear
This all seems overwhelming
A good day is oh so rare.

But in the middle of this party
Of this pity and the blues
Have you ever taken out your mirror?
To reflect it might be you?

It may be results of choices
Or what you sow you reap
It may be what you did today
Before you went to sleep.

Wandering Journey

It might be blinders that you're wearing
That block your vision and your sight
It might be that the halo upon your head
Is just a little tight.

So before you make your guest list
And start the music of the blues
It might be the way you're living
And the style of life you choose.

If you can relate to this message
Or if it hits a nerve today
It may be time to get on your knees
To our God it's time to pray.

For His *spirit dwells in* you
Surrender all to God above
Ask Him for forgiveness
And lots and lots of love.

And soon you'll find that party
You have no need or time to spend
Because it's all behind you
When Christ became your friend.

Thanks Be To God

Help me Father, for my vision to be
Thankful for blessings given to me.

Getting up in the morning, tired and slow
Thank you God that at least I can go.

When the toast burns and the coffee is weak
Help me God for thy blessings to seek.

When I grumble because my shower's not hot,
Help me "see" all that I've got.

When the clothes are dirty, and there's wash to do
Thank you for family, that comes from you.

When the traffic is slow, and I'm really late
Thank you for the minute that I have to wait.

When the day is chaos and all seems wild
Thank you for comfort, peace, and mild.

When my sandwich is dry and my drink is not cold
Thank you for food, and the blessings you hold.

When I come home tired, worn out from the day
Thank you for children and all that they say.

When I'm washing the dishes, the pots and pans
Thank you for sight, and hard working hands.

When helping with homework, getting kids ready for bed
Thank you for thoughts, a mind, and a clear head.

When we pray together, and snuggle up tight,
Thank you for rest and the quiet of the night.

Oh God help me see what's real and what's true,
That our blessings are plenty, and given from you.

Wandering Journey

As I come to you daily and thank you for bread,
Thank you for Jesus, and the Words that He said.

Please clean my heart, my soul, and my mind.
Slow down; breathe in, for the blessings to find.

Oh God, help me be your child as I live.
To be thankful and sharing, willing to give.

To share and to love, to hug and to smile!
To be willing to lend, walk that extra mile.

I pray to you now, Oh God who is the King!
Thank you for all the blessings you bring!

Because

Because of Easter morning
That Jesus gave us all,
The gift to each was given
When He took for us the fall.

Because of Easter morning
All the sins and grievances you bare
Can be laid out and forgiven
Because Jesus did His share.

Because of Easter morning
We can love instead of hate
We see bright and new beginnings
Instead of dread and fate.

Because of Easter morning
We see good in a fellow man
Instead of criticizing judgment
We reach out a helping hand.

Because of Easter morning
We forgive others and put behind
The hurt, the pain, and the suffering
And soon the peace we find.

Because of Easter morning
We want to tell the news!
To all of those who may not know
There is so much to lose!

Because of Easter morning
Death has lost its sting
As Jesus gave us life again
In heaven we will sing!

Because of Easter morning
Life is worth living everyday
Praise God our living Savior
Let our hearts and voices say.

Because of Easter morning
The free gift given for us all
All because of Jesus Christ
Who took for us, the fall!

The Perfect Christmas

Oh, the perfect Christmas, is so very hard to find,
To get it just so perfect is a stress that works your mind.

We want to give the perfect gift, we search rushing here and there,
Struggling though crowds of people, who seem neither polite nor fair.

We have all kind of parties, the preparation is intense,
The guests arrive, we entertain, we stay stressed and very tense.

We're bombarded on all corners of what Christmas is supposed to be,
The sales, the dress, to look good, what a chaotic scene to see.

We send our gifts all over, in packages wrapped so tight,
Our cards flood the busy mail, what a busy bustling sight.

We want to look just dazzling, to match the season's scene,
Dress up and smile, be happy now, it's in the season's theme.

Does this all seem a little shallow? You don't feel like it's all right?
You feel like something's missing, when you go to bed at night?

That's because we're missing what Advent is all about,
Remember key words given, to follow the right route.

Of PEACE that is given, to know God's in control.
He loves and cares, we are saved, Christ saved our very soul.

Of LOVE from God our Father, and love that we can share.
To care and love each other, Oh Christ! You are so fair!

There is JOY to know about the gift, that God shared with us from above,
Jesus, the child savior, was born for us, with love.

And HOPE we have because of faith, a new life for you and me.
Hope for us, each day to day, oh what a vision for us to see.

So make your Christmas priority, to prepare your heart and mind.
To witness God's visit here, that Christ, you may truly find.

Prepare your heart, prepare your soul, and reach close to God each day,
Accept the perfect gift of Christ, for He is the only way.

So there you have it! Christmas time, that's what should be in the season
HOPE, JOY, PEACE, and always LOVE, remember Jesus is the reason.

Love

We think of love with sweets and cards
Pretty flowers, notes, and hearts.
With chocolates and candy kisses galore
And little people shooting darts.

But God has created a real love,
One that cannot compare
Without holiday of sugar and sweets
A love that really shares!

The love you feel when you hold your child
And look at the sweet innocent face.
You're moved and love surges through your heart
And you thank God for His wonderful grace.

The love you feel when you reach out
To someone who is in pain
When life's not right, it's all a mess!
You care, and help them keep sane.

The love of this creation!
So beautiful and bright!
The stars, the moon, the ocean deep!
Oh what an awesome sight.

The love that happens when you say "I do"
To the person you decided to keep
As your soul mate, spouse, and your best friend
You know, what you sow, you'll reap.

The love of our Father and His soul
The greatest love ever given
Return it to God and Jesus his Son
And you will someday meet in heaven.

What Was It Like?

What was it like on that Christmas Eve?
To be there and experience it all?
What was it like on that starry night
For Mary, when she answered God's call?

Confusion or fear? Traveling with child
Discomfort, and yet she was able
To give birth to a child, heavenly conceived
On the ground, on the hay, in a stable.

What was it like for Joseph that night?
Who wondered, but stayed true to Mary
To help birth a child, in the cold and the hay
What a load for a young man to carry.

What was it like for shepherds at work?
In the night, a frightening type scene
Of angels to come announcing a birth
Were they not stunned, at heavenly beings?

What was it like for God to share
His Son, with us humans on earth
When He knew the outcome and what we would bring
Was it hard to bring forth this birth?

What was it like, for Jesus the babe
Did He know what the plan was to be?
Do you think of the ultimate Gift that was given
And the blood for you that was shed.

What was it like? We don't know for sure
But we do know what Christmas does bring
Our salvation from sin, and eternal life
For that let us joyfully sing!

Sing with praises like Mary
Have faith, like Joseph in God's word
Seek out the gift, like the shepherds
Rejoice like the angels, so it is heard!

On This Day

Today as you're walking down the aisle
Stepping onto an untouched way.
Making a life changing decision
By what your about to say.

Marriage is a decision
A decision of unending love.
No matter what happens in the future
Your promise is to each other and above.

So don't take these vows lightly
Listen! Hear the words that are said
When God hears promises from his children
He expects them to follow where he's led.

To love, no matter what happens,
To forgive and to understand
To think the best and be caring
Always willing to reach out your hand.

To forgive when the other has stumbled
To love when one is sick or down.
To hang in there when the ocean is tossing
And sometimes listen, without making a sound.

To stick together when the world around you
Is tempting and saying bail out!
To cling tightly, holding forever
Even when there's a shadow of doubt.

The secret to this kind of existence
Is simple as simple can be.
You must ask God and our Savior
To center you life, don't you see?

You must seek God first and follow
Then love your spouse without end.
God will guide and instruct you
Always giving a hand to lend.

Wandering Journey

A marriage centered on Jesus
Will hold firm and continually grow
A relationship's solid foundation
Enables the love to flow.

So remember this day forever
As you join together for life.
Make God the center of everything
As you become husband and wife.

What If Jesus Had Not Come?

Think if we had no Christmas, and Jesus had not been born
There was no Christmas Eve, or waking on Christmas morn.

If Christmas was just another day, we got up and went on with life,
Struggling with no future, but pain, sin, and strife.

What if we had no Christmas, no carols or joyous songs,
No hope for eternal life, just the drudgery of what we've done wrong.

If we had no friend in Jesus, no stories of Christ to tell,
No Easter, no savior or miracles, of Jesus who made the sick well.

What if we had no love, no joy, or peace or hope,
No counselor to guide us along, and help with out troubles to cope.

What would have happened if God did not care, and had left us alone on this earth!
We didn't have Isaiah or prophets, who predicted the Savior's birth.

The good news is we do have Christmas, as God loves and cares for us so
He did send us a savior, His grace and mercy he shows.

He gave us a ticket to heaven, with no charge or fee to admit
Only a humble and repenting heart and a dedicated life to commit.

A future filled with joy, hope, and peace continuing with no end
His spirit, angels, and his guidance are always available to send.

So rejoice at this Christmas season, it's a life changing event for us all
He sent Jesus, who will always love us, after all He has taken our fall.

Thirty Three Years

Oh! See the tiny hands of the baby that lies
So small in the manger, his mother she prays

She holds him and cuddles her sweet little child
The night is so calm, so peaceful and mild

The milk that he drinks, from his mother so dear
Nourishes his small body, he has no fears

The angels are singing, celebrating the night
The brightness, the star, our morning light

The shepherds are looking, the king to see
At the awesome sight of God's Son, a tiny baby

The swaddling clothes wrapped snugly and tight
Keep him safe and warm on a chilly clear night

The animals surround him, all peaceful and calm
As the child is given and rests in God's palm

But then it all changes after thirty three years
A couple of miles from this spot, there is a shedding of tears

The sweet little hands are now pierced with a nail
As the blood flows freely, and people mockingly hail

He's not cuddled or coddled, but hanging in pain
By people who curse him and see that he's slain

There is no milk to nourish, so sweet and so fine
To sooth a parched throat, just sour wine

No one is singing, the sun goes away
It seems like the night, in the mid of the day

No shepherds, no gifts, just spitting and hate
As the crowd gathers round, to see Jesus's fate

Wandering Journey

No swaddling clothes, wrapped snugly or nice,
But ripped off and gambled for with a set of dice

No animals no calm or quietness or peace,
But angry people, crucify, Jesus' life to cease

What a difference those years made, like night and day,
All for us sinners, Jesus, our debt to pay

God had a plan, a new promise to save
A new way of salvation, He had already paved

So on this Christmas of presents, of joy and sweets,
Let's bow on our knees to our Father, at His feet.

For God gave us our Savior on Christmas was born
But on Good Friday His life ended shattered and torn

Jesus suffered for us, for each old and small
All part of God's plan He answered His call

God bless you today; keep God in your heart
God's gift saved your future, *from* Him never part

Keep your life together by following His diving plan
Love God, love Jesus, and love each other, all that you can.

www.ingramcontent.com/pod-product-compliance
Lightning Source LLC
Chambersburg PA
CBHW051805040426
42446CB00007B/519